MASKS of the KORANKO PORO

Form, Function and Comparison to the Toma

OTHER WORKS BY THIS AUTHOR

FROM ETHNOS PUBLICATIONS

———————————

MAKING THE GRADE: THE MEANING OF METALS IN PORO ART OF WEST AFRICA

COMPARATIVE NATIVE TERMINOLOGY OF PORO GROUPS

BAKOROGI MASKS OF THE LOMA

PORO, POWER AND POISON: UNDERSTANDING THE WEST AFRICAN SECRET SOCIETY THROUGH ART

Neil Carey

MASKS of the KORANKO PORO

Form, Function and Comparison to the Toma

ETHNOS
PUBLICATIONS
AMHERST, MA

After all, what would be the value of the passion for knowledge if it resulted only in a certain amount of knowledgeableness and not, in one way or another and to the extent possible, in the knower's straying afield of himself? There are times in life when the question of knowing if one can think differently than one thinks, and perceive differently than one sees, is absolutely necessary if one is to go on looking and reflecting at all. People will say, perhaps, that these games with oneself would better be left backstage; or, at best, that they might properly form part of those preliminary exercises that are forgotten once they have served their purpose. But, then, what is philosophy today – philosophical activity, I mean – if it is not the critical work that thought brings to bear on itself? In what does it consist, if not in the endeavor to know how and to what extent it might be possible to think differently, instead of legitimating what is already known?

–Michel Foucault

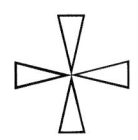

Contents

xi	Acknowledgments
xiii	List of Illustrations
15	A Brief Overview of Poro Masking Traditions
17	The Koranko
19	Masks of the Koranko Poro
20	The Boys' Poro Mask
21	The Men's Poro Mask
23	The Elders' Poro Mask
25	The Toma
26	Comparison of Koranko and Toma Masks
36	An Enigma: The Stone Mask
39	A Revisitation of Published Examples
50	Stylistic Variations
52	Summary
53	Notes
59	References
63	Index

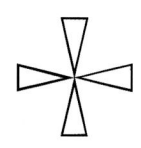

Acknowledgements

The following scenario illustrates the difficulties facing a Westerner trying to decipher Poro art. Imagine if you will, attending a military convention where all levels, from raw recruit to four-star general, were present from each branch of service. If you had previously been initiated into a military association such as the army or air force, you might be able to distinguish between most ranks of your own branch, e.g. private first class, lieutenant, ensign or captain. But how could you be expected to identify all those myriad people in their variously colored and styled uniforms? Why does one wear white with an odd collar and white cap while another wears blue with gold trim on his hat? What are those oak leaf clusters and what do they mean, and aren't those shoulder stripes pretty? Yet, to the upper echelons, all this is second nature.

Now imagine the even greater difficulty in making sense of all this for an African native who, having lived his entire life in the bush, is suddenly thrust into this foreign milieu. Totally confused, he might devise all kinds of entertaining theories by dividing the various military personnel into artificial "types" according to the color of their shoes, or even the type of metal used for their belt buckles. To compound his problem, suppose the military people had been trained from youth to keep everything regarding the military totally secret, on pain of death.

This is the situation in which I found myself ten years ago, when beginning my Poro studies. After the seminal works of George Way Harley and George Schwab, the literature became confusing and in some cases, quite inaccurate. This situation was undoubtedly due to the successful use by the Poro of deception, denial and distraction to hide their secrets. It is truly the quintessential secret society. It became apparent to me that the only way to obtain even a glimmer of the inner workings of the Poro association and its rituals was to receive honest instruction from a knowledgeable Poro initiate.

Like Alexander Fleming and his penicillium mold, I serendipitously met my Liberian associate M.S. Aboudoulaye just when my interest in the Poro was sprouting. "Abe" was initiated into the Poro of the Mano in northeast Liberia. Having trained under his mentor "Baba" Talibi Kaba (who worked for years with Dr. George Harley), he assisted Liberian museums and well-known American and German ethnographers. Mr. Aboudoulaye is indeed a "walking encyclopedia" of Poro, having a broad first-hand knowledge of Poro rituals in Sierra Leone, Guinea, Liberia and Côte d'Ivoire. I am forever indebted to him for his willingness to "spill the beans."

My appeciation must be expressed to my Loma associate Gabriel of Lawalazu, Liberia, who was initiated into the Poro of his people.

Thanks are also due to K. Scott Rodolitz, currently the specialist in charge of the Department of

African and Oceanic Art at Bonhams New York for his assistance. I am indebted to Diane Pelrine, Curator of the Arts of Africa, Oceania and the Americas, Indiana University Art Museum, for her efforts to provide images of the fine mask at IUAM, and to Susan Grinois, of the Fine Arts Museums of San Francisco, who likewise provided the photograph of the mask from the de Young Museum. Petra Felder of Zemanek-Münster kindly provided the image from their catalogue. Thanks are due to Susan Haskell and Julie Brown of Harvard's Peabody Museum for their efforts in trying to provide a higher resolution image of their mask, and also to Austin Kennedy of Pace Primitive and Rebecca Akan of the Metropolitan Museum of Art for their attempts to locate the current location of the mask published in Rubin's 1974 book African Accumulative Sculpture.

Dr. Neil Carey

List of Illustrations

18	Figure 1. Map: The Koranko Territory in Sierra Leone and Guinea.
20	Figure 2. Poro Terminology of the Koranko and Loma
21	Figure 3. Mask of the Koranko Boy's Poro.
22	Figure 4. Mask of the Koranko Men's Poro.
22	Figure 5. Scarification patterns of the Boys' and Men's Poro
24	Figure 6. Mask of the Koranko Elders' Poro.
25	Figure 7. Map: Language groups in Guinea.
27	Figure 8. *Masgui*, the supreme Bush Spirit of the Toma.
28	Figure 9. Toma *Buzogi* horizontal mask.
28	Figure 10. A Poro *Zo* demonstrating how the Toma *Buzogi* mask is worn.
29	Figure 11. A Toma *Angbai* mask from the Elders' Poro.
30	Figure 12. A Toma *Angbai* horizontal mask.
31	Figure 13. A Toma *Landai* horizontal mask.
32	Figure 14. Rear view of Toma *Landai* mask.
32	Figure 15. A Toma *Landai* mask in full costume.
33	Figure 16. A Toma masquerader wearing *Landai* mask.
34	Figure 17. A Loma miniature mask.
35	Figure 18. *Kwo Wale,* a figural urn of a Loma *Zo*.
38	Figure 19. An ancient stone mask, probably Koranko.
40	Figure 20. A Koranko Boys' Poro mask.
41	Figure 21. A Koranko Boys' Poro mask.
42	Figure 22. A Koranko Elders' Poro mask.
42	Figure 23. A Koranko mask from the Men's Poro.
43	Figure 24. A Koranko Boys' Poro body mask.
44	Figure 25. A five-horned Koranko mask from the Men's Poro.
45	Figure 26. A Koranko Boys' Poro body mask.

46	Figure 27. A Koranko Boys' Poro mask.
47	Figure 28. A Koranko Boys' Poro mask.
48	Figure 29. A Koranko Men's Poro body mask.
49	Figure 30. A Koranko Men's Poro body mask.

A Brief Overview of Poro Masking Traditions

Generically called the "Poro" secret society by Western observers, this men's association is widespread throughout the Guinea Coast of West Africa. An integral part of the traditional religion of the region, Poro has existed, according to some scholars, for at least 2,500 years (Korvah 1995: 91; Migeod 1916, Johnson 1974), long before the multiple waves of migration occurred that brought the present inhabitants to Sierra Leone, Liberia, Guinea and Côte d'Ivoire. Regardless of its age, Poro has undoubtedly influenced cultures in this area for many, many centuries.

The social-religious-political role of the Poro in maintaining social control and preserving the status quo[1] has had varying degrees of success in preventing "new religions" –Christianity and Islam – from making inroads into sub-Saharan West Africa. Although evolution over the centuries has resulted in distinct variations in the Poro of different groups, and while there may be only vestiges of Poro remaining in some areas, there persists today a comprehensive organization with similar structure and function throughout the Guinea Coast. Different peoples, even within the same language group, often use different names for their own particular Poro associations. This author has found more than thirty different local names for Poro that have been recorded in the literature, from six language groups, and it is suspected that some peoples on the fringes of present day Poro country may still be practicing in some fashion (Carey 2007a). Poro is a generic term for the society, and is used throughout this work.

One of the shared characteristics of all Poro groups is the presence of a strong masking tradition, in which Bush Spirits or "Bush Devils", embodied in masks, are controlled through esoteric knowledge, sacrifices and rituals by powerful medicine men (called *Zoes* among many Mande and Kruan speakers). Unlike the masquerades of many other groups, in which the masker is understood by the observer to be a human in costume *representing* a spirit, a Poro mask, whether it is danced or not, actually *is* a Bush Spirit, with its own particular authority and power.

Among the various styles of Poro masks found throughout the region are the familiar face masks of the Dan, Mano, and Kono, the forehead masks of the Bassa, the horizontal masks of the Kpelle, Kissi, Gbandi and Loma (Toma)[2], the helmet masks of the Gola and Senufo, and unworn masks made of wood, metal and even stone. Regardless of how a Poro mask is anatomically worn, it is still a Bush Spirit, living somewhere in the hierarchy of that particular group's masking tradition.

Another characteristic common to all Poro associations is a hierarchy of the organization based upon not only age groups but also upon the possession of increasing levels of esoteric knowledge. Although there are minor variations among groups, the basic structure of the Poro consists of three levels.

First comes the Boys' Poro, in which pubescent boys are sequestered in the Sacred Bush (also referred to as the Sacred Grove) outside of the village for sometimes up to seven years. During their stay in the Bush School they are circumcised[3] if the procedure has not already been performed. Then they are scarified, taught secret codes and secret language, swear oaths against revealing Poro secrets, learn Poro laws and customs, and are taught the skills of farming, hut building, hunting, warfare and sexual conduct. The initiates enter the Bush as children, but leave as responsible adult members of the community.

Next comes the Men's Poro, in which deeper levels of esoteric knowledge and Poro secrets are learned. It has its own initiation rituals, including further scarification on the arms and torso. The Men assume certain increased responsibilities, including civic duties.

Ultimately, a man might be initiated into the upper echelon, the Elders' Poro, which in some groups required a human sacrifice. Consisting of powerful *Zoes*, the Elders' Poro in most (but not all) groups has political power even over the secular Paramount Chief.

Each level of Poro has its own distinct panoply of masks, each one with its own specific style and function. Some masks might be seen both publicly by the villagers including uninitiated males, women and even outsiders, as well as within the secret confines of the Sacred Bush. In this case, the secret names and roles of these masks inside the Bush might be very different from their public ones. Other Bush Spirit masks, particularly most of the powerful masks of the Elders' Poro, are *never* seen outside of the Sacred Bush, and sometimes are not even revealed to members of the two lower levels.

From the very first day of their initiations, Poro members swear oaths to protect Poro secrets. The penalty for revealing secrets about Poro business is death by poisoning. Jackson notes that Koranko boys are first taught secret signs and code words as early as age 8-10, when, still uninitiated, they join semi-formal play groups called the *Tulbare* and *Gbongbokode* in preparation for, and anticipation of, Poro initiation (Jackson 1977: 224). This all-pervasive and well-entrenched secrecy among Poro groups has been well documented[4], and is undoubtedly the reason behind much of the confusion in the current literature. For example, because Dan Poro initiates were so highly successful in hiding the association's very existence to outsiders, two German ethnographers concluded in error that there is no Poro among the Dan people (Fischer and Himmelheber 1984:103). In a similar fashion, Jackson, a New Zealander who did much excellent field work among the Koranko in 1969 and 1971, never saw, nor was he informed of, any masking tradition connected to their associations. Hence, he concluded that, "carved masks are unknown among the Kuranko" (Jackson 1977a: 236 note 23).

The Koranko

However, there does exist an unusual style of mask that is found among the Koranko (Kuranko, Kouranko), a Mande-speaking people living in a very sparsely populated mountainous region of the western and northwestern Guinea Highlands (Figure 1). The Koranko, mainly subsistence farmers, are a branch of the Mandinka group. Their origins have been traced back to the Mande Empire, whose power influenced much of the West Sudan in the thirteenth and fourteenth centuries (Jackson 1974:398). They are thought to have migrated into their present area from the north, pushed by invaders, in about 1600 CE. The 1963 Sierra Leone census reported that the total Koranko population was over 125,000, with about 80,732 living in Sierra Leone. In the early 1990's it was about 270,000 (Olson,1996). However, in light of the recent conflicts in Sierra Leone, Liberia and Guinea, their present numbers and distribution are not known.

Unlike their Mandinka ancestors, most Koranko are still practicing their traditional religion, having been very resistant to inroads of the "new religions" – Islam and Christianity. Today they are found primarily in Sierra Leone and in the northern Kissidougou area of Guinea (Paulme 1954: Fig. 1 (map); Foray 1977:113-114; O'Toole 1995). In Guinea, the eastern margin of Koranko territory extends as far as Beyla, where they are bordered by the Toma (the Loma people living on the Guinea side of the border with Liberia), whereas their southern neighbors are the Kissi (Jackson 1977a: 3). In Sierra Leone, Koranko land is bordered by the Kono, Temne and Limba. All these groups – the Toma, Kissi, Kono, Temne, Limba and Koranko– possess their own variants of Poro, each with its own associated local masking styles, traditions and local Poro vocabulary (see Figure 2).

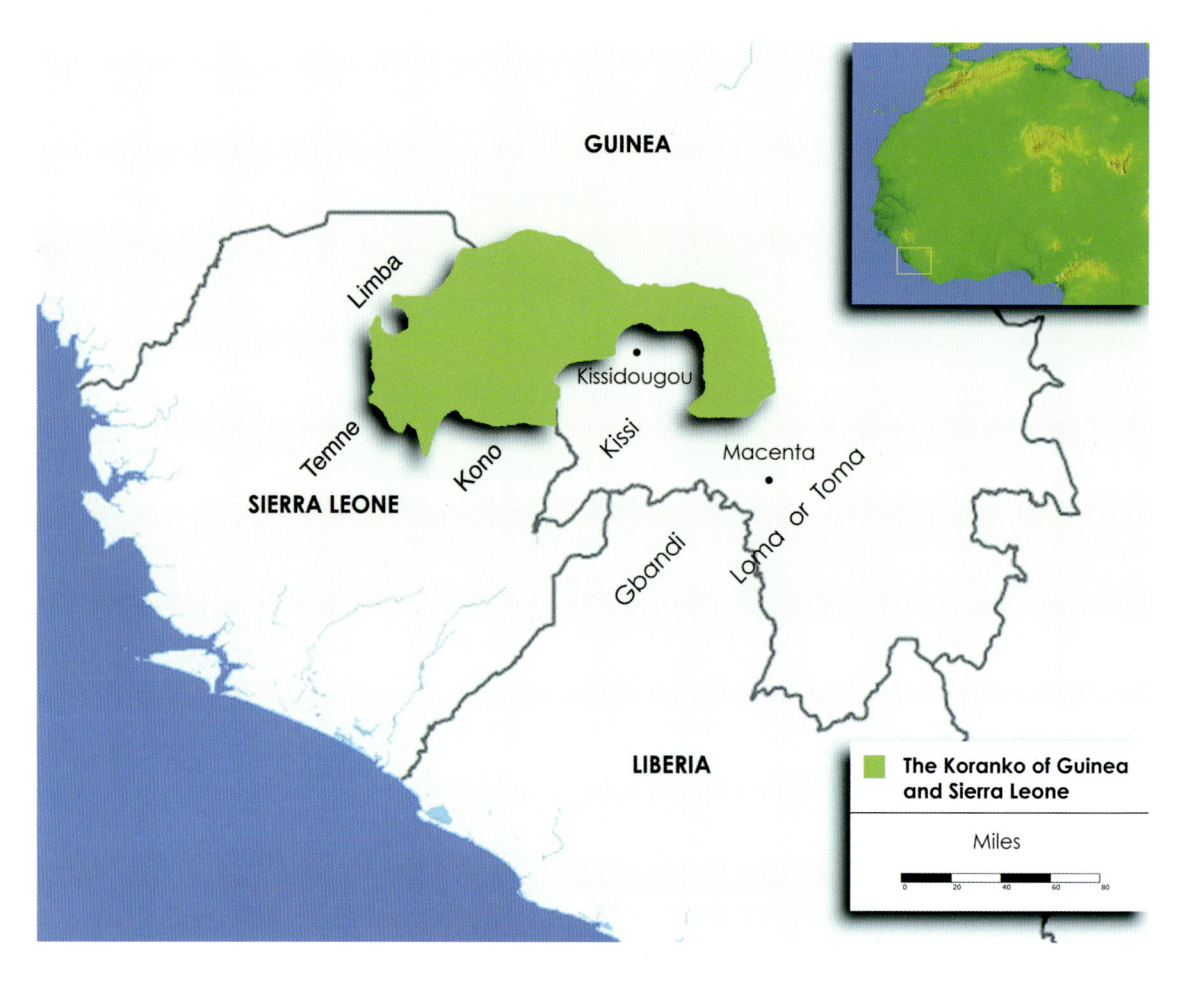

Figure 1. The Koranko Territory in Sierra Leone and Guinea.

The Koranko straddle the Sierra Leone-Guinea border and inhabit an area just north of the point where the borders of Guinea, Sierra Leone, and Liberia meet. In the far eastern extension of their territory, they are neighbors of the Toma and Kissi to their south. The western half of Koranko land in Sierra Leone is bordered by the Temne, Limba and Kono. All these groups have well-documented Poro. (Map by N. Carey).

Masks of the Koranko Poro

Among the corpus of masks from this region of Guinea that have been described in the literature or have appeared in public and private collections, most have been attributed to the Toma (Loma), with a very small number being attributed to the Gbandi and the Kissi. Within this group, however, a small number of masks exist that share a commonality of form that is quite distinct from that of the Loma (Toma), Kissi and Gbandi. This form is determined in part by the method in which the masks are worn. These masks are from the Koranko, and are used in their Poro rituals.

To begin, the following describes a complete set of *Gah'* masks[5] from the Poro association (variously called *Gbangbami*[6], *Gbangbe*, *Kome* or *Andomba*[9]) of the Koranko people living in Guinea, coming from the hinterland between the Toma and the Northern Kissi. These are body masks, and are worn by the masquerader affixed to his back in a vertical position.[7] All three masks date from the first quarter of the 20th century, and their attachments have been replaced throughout the years. This set is original and complete, and is quite important, as it comes from all three levels of Poro (Boys', Men's and Elders'), is all from the same Koranko village or Poro camp, and displays the stylistic elements which visually distinguish between each grade in their Poro hierarchy.

Like all Poro masks, these are Bush Spirits. Unlike many other cultures wherein the observer understands the masquerader to be a human in costume *representing* a spirit, Poro masks, whether worn, danced or simply displayed, *are* the Bush Spirits incarnate in the object. The mask and the masker are one.

The generic term for a Koranko Bush Spirit is *Nyenne* (Jackson, 1977a p. 34-35, 225). A *Nyenne* mask is worn by a powerful medicine man (*Kometigi, Gbongbane*) belonging to the upper levels of Poro. It might never be seen outside the confines of the Sacred Bush (*Komebon*). This is parallel to Poro-related *Gɛ* (Bush Spirit) masks among the Dan being worn by a *Zo* in the *Gɛ Bo* (Harley (1941:7-8), or the *Ga* masks of the Mano worn by their *Zo* in the secluded *Bo Kpoa* (Schwab, 1947 p. 246).

Kome is one name for the Koranko Poro association and is the name of "a powerful and dangerous bush spirit" (Jackson, 1977a p. 34-35, 225). Jackson speaks of the *Kome* and the *Gbangbe* as two separate cult associations. However, he seems to be describing the same organizational structure and function as other Poro groups, wherein different *Zoes* (or in the Koranko tongue the *Kometigi* and the *Gbongbane*) specialize in different skills, and the hierarchy is based on age levels, possession of esoteric knowledge, and the relative strength of medicines. In this case, *Kome* appears to be a specific Bush Spirit who enforces social control through the administration of potent biological and chemical agents (Jackson knew of three types) and through the knowledge and control of antidotes. This is also descriptive of the "judgment masks" of other Poro groups with their various local names.

Gbangbe (per Jackson) has "more secretiveness and seriousness", and unlike the *Kome*, it never has public displays. This suggests that *Gbangbe* is also a distinct Bush Spirit, with its own mask. One can draw a parallel between the *Gbangbe* and those very powerful masked Bush Spirits in other Poro groups, which are seen only within the confines of the Sacred Bush, and sometimes only by the Elders' Poro.

Figure 2. Poro Terminology of the Koranko and Loma (from Carey 2007)

ETHNIC GROUP	LANGUAGE GROUP	NATIVE NAME FOR THE PORO SOCIETY	GENERIC NAME FOR BUSH SPIRIT/MASK	SUPREME PORO BUSH SPIRIT/MASK	NATIVE TERM FOR MEDICINE MAN[77]	NATIVE NAME FOR THE SACRED BUSH
Koranko	Mande	Gbangbe[13, 14], Kome[14], Gbangbami[15], Andomba[25]	Kome, Nyenne[14], ŋina[16]	Komah'h[7]	Kometigi, Gbongbane[14], Basi ti[16]	Komebon[14]
Loma	Mande	Poro[17, 18], Polo, Pölögii[19]	Mã[5]	Masgui[7]	Zo, Dazoe[20], Zowī[21], Zòwò[22], Kolou Zowoi[23]	Gɛbɔ, Gɛbo[7], Savei[76]

The Boys' Poro Mask

The simplest mask from the set of three is the mask from the Boys' Poro (Figure 3). It is 30 inches high (77 cm), and is carved from a single piece of dense wood to which has been attached animal horns, cowry shells, iron, red cloth (signifying Poro), glass mirrors, power materials and accumulated sacrificial residue. The Boys' level is indicated by the one phallic central horn, which is surrounded by the two inwardly curved horns of the animal that must be sacrificed to it. Other Boys' masks sometimes have only the two outer horns. This mask is present at the *Birike*, the initiation ritual of the young boys when they first enter the Sacred Bush. Powerful "medicine" lies underneath the circular cloth cap that is tied onto the forehead above the mirrored eyes. It is thought that this refers to the small hats worn by the boys upon initiation, a common tradition among many Poro groups.

Figure 3. Mask of the Koranko Boy's Poro.
Guinea
Wood, animal horns, cowry shells, iron, red cloth, mirrors, power materials and accumulated sacrificial residue.
Height 30 inches (77 cm)
1st quarter of the 20th century.
Private collection.
Often attributed to the Toma, the Koranko Boys' Poro mask can be differentiated by its shallow planar form with a flat underside, enabling it to be worn flush against the masquerader's body. The three horns carved on the top of the head (two in some examples) indicate that this belongs to the Boys' level. (Photograph by N. Carey).

The Men's Poro Mask

Even larger and more complex is the body mask from the Men's Poro (Figure 4). It is 31 inches high (78 cm), and, like the mask from the Boys' Poro, is carved from a single piece of wood, upon which are attached antelope horns, red cloth, glass mirrors, power material and accumulated sacrificial material. It is an oath taking figure as well as a mask. There are five horns: the animal to be sacrificed is symbolized by the outer pair, the arms that will be cut (scarified) during the men's initiation by the inner pair, and the scarifications on the men's upper body by the central horn (refer to Fig. 5) [8.] The edge of the face has a distinctive bevel found on several other Koranko masks. A smiling mouth is shallowly incised on the lower face.

Figure 4. Mask of the Koranko Men's Poro
Guinea
Wood, antelope horns, red cloth, glass mirrors, power material and accumulated sacrificial material.
Height 31 inches (78 cm)
1st quarter of the 20th century
Private collection.
Of overall similar construction as the Boys' Poro mask, the increase to five horns communicates that this mask is more powerful, and belongs to the Men's level of Poro.
(Photograph by N. Carey).

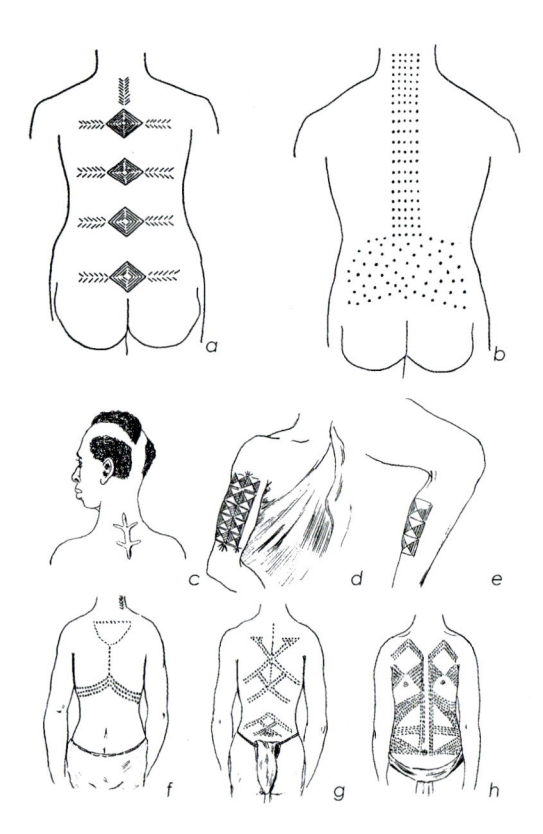

Figure 5. Scarification patterns of the Boys' and Men's Poro of neighboring groups.[8]
Among the Koranko, torso scarification on adult initiates is represented by the middle horn of the Men's Poro mask while arm scarification is represented by the inner pair of horns. Loma (Toma) man (*a*, *b*, *f* and *h*); Gbandi man (*c*); Kissi man (*d* and *e*) and boy (*h*). (Drawing from Schwab 1947:119, and Germann 1933: Plate 3).

The Elders' Poro Mask

The largest and most complex mask is from the Elders' Poro (Figure 6). It is 38 inches high (95 cm), and upon it are attached animal horns, cowry shells, iron, red cloth, mirrored glass, power materials and accumulated sacrificial residue. The Elders' mask is not worn. It is the central and most sacred object for the entire Koranko Poro. The old men make all vows upon it, and use it to make themselves strong by praying to it.

This particular example has twelve horns carved atop its head in three ranks of increasing size: two in the front row, four larger ones in the second row, and the six largest horns curving concentrically towards the centerline in the third row. The overall form is of a three-tiered structure, of which the two, four and six-horned layers are stacked one against the other like the layers of a wedding cake. One could surmise that this arrangement refers to the three levels of Poro, but the meaning of the actual number of horns is unknown outside of the Elders.

Of particular interest is the shallow concavity in the back of the largest tier. Unlike the simple flat plank of the Boys' and Men's masks, where the attachment holes are bored from the front to the rear, the concavity of the Elders' mask creates sides to the mask. The holes are therefore bored through the *sides*, not the front. This is a peculiar feature of the Elders' mask, and should not be misconstrued as indicating that this mask is worn horizontally on the head like Toma masks; as noted, the Elders' mask is not worn at all. A similar form is found in the Elders' mask in Figure 23.

The smallest, front-most tier with the two smallest horns on top acts as the forehead of this overall abstract mask. To this are affixed two hanging, semicircular animal horns, creating an almost complete circle. These horns are filled with various power materials, most likely animal and/or human parts, metal, poison, or other "medicines". In the center of this lies a small, round mirror almost hidden under a coating of accumulated sacrificial material, and this, in turn, is surrounded by a circle of cowry shells. Mirrors, a powerful and magical medicine, are also found on some masks of the Loma Poro. Dangling down from the apex of the circle of horns is a small antelope horn filled with medicine and sealed with a wrapping of red (the color of Poro) fabric. There is only a tiny nose. The opening in the trumpet-like mouth penetrates through to the inside of the mask.

Figure 6. Mask of the Koranko Elders' Poro
Guinea
Wood, animal horns, cowry shells, iron, red cloth, mirrored glass, power materials and accumulated sacrificial material. Height 38 inches (95 cm).
1st quarter of the 20th century.
Private collection.
This large and heavy mask belongs to the Elders' level of Poro, as indicated by the twelve carved horns atop the head. Of a more complex, layered structure than the masks of the lower grades, it is not worn. (Photograph by N. Carey).

The Toma

The Loma people who live just across the Liberian border in Guinea are administratively called Toma, though they refer to themselves as Loma. Culturally they are the same, although as expected, there are stylistic differences in the sculpture throughout their range, in part due to influences of the neighboring Koranko, Gbandi and Guerzé (the Guinea Kpelle). The mountainous Toma land abuts Koranko territory only at its extreme southeastern "tail" in Guinea (see Figure 7).

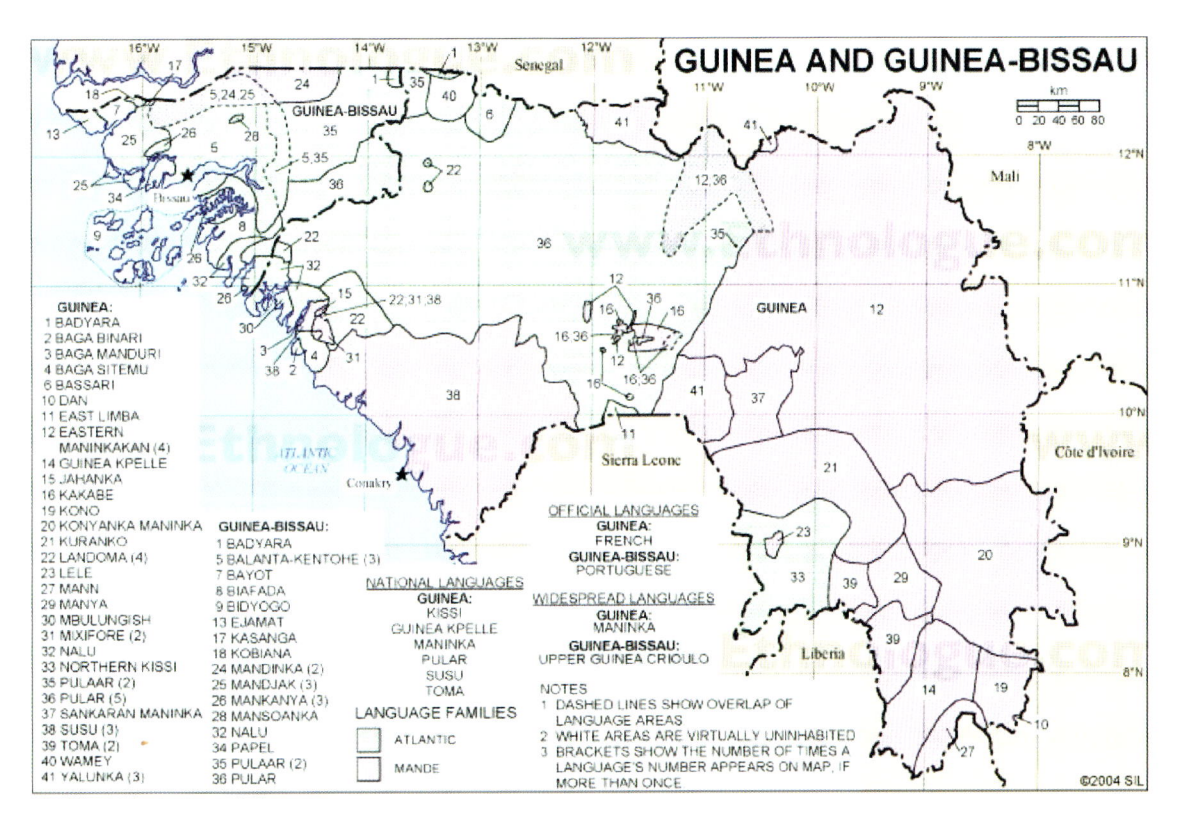

Figure 7. Language groups in Guinea. The Toma (area 39) border the Koranko (area 21) in only one small area at the extreme tip of the "tail" of Koranko land. (From: Gordon 2005).

25

Comparison of Koranko and Toma Masks

The Poro of the Koranko and the Toma (*Polo, Pölögii*) both make and use Bush Spirit masks in a hierarchical masking tradition. However, a mask's identity and its place in the masking hierarchy are displayed in different ways. Amongst the Koranko, it is the *number* of horns, plus the addition of power material, that stylistically communicates increasing status and power of Bush Spirit masks. Amongst the Toma, it is the actual *form* of the horns and mask rather than the number, plus the addition of power material, that indicates its identity and strength.

Figure 8 shows the paramount mask of the Toma, their Supreme (Bush) Spirit. All Poro power derives ultimately from this great mask, called *Masgui* (Grandfather). It is the most holy center of the Poro Elders, and is used for all their most sacred purposes. The mask is not worn, but is kept within the secret confines of the Poro society Sacred Grove, where it is propped between the buttress roots of a sacred old cotton tree. Sacrifices are made and oaths are taken upon it, and blood from the sacrificed animals is kept in the small pot atop the head. During the circumcision rites, a bowl is used to collect all the boys' spilt blood, which is then placed on the top of the mask as an offering, before the blood is made into a stew. The iron on the head is called *benzue*, and is powerful medicine. The jar is used as a poison oracle as well (Carey 2008, plate 97).

Masgui is of a very large rectangular form. Unlike Koranko masks, the hierarchical status of *Masgui* is indicated by its *form* and by the attached power materials. The Koranko paramount mask, called *Komah*, is the twelve-horned Elders' mask seen here in Figure 6, but with a much greater quantity of encrusted power material. Like the *Masgui*, it is not worn.

Probably because of their large size and planar form, Koranko body masks are usually attributed to the neighboring Toma, whose large flat masks are most commonly (but not always) worn horizontally atop the head (see Figures 8 – 17). This confusion is most likely due to the relatively few Koranko masks in Western collections and their lack of accompanying collection data, plus the proximity of the Koranko to the Toma. This situation is akin to that of other Poro groups along the Guinea coast, where it is almost guaranteed that museum and auction catalogs will attribute Mano and Kono masks to the Dan, and attribute Kru and Sapo masks to the Kran (Guéré).

Figure 8. *Masgui*, the supreme Bush Spirit of the Toma.
Lissaou-Macenta, Guinea
Wood with iron, terracotta, blood, sacrificial materials and remains of red and blue pigments.
Date: 19th century
Private collection
Masgui is not worn, but leaned against a sacred cotton tree between its buttress roots in the Sacred Grove. (Photograph by N. Carey).

The forms of the Loma horizontal mask and the Koranko body mask are consistent with their usage, however. Loma masks are carved with significant concavity on the bottom side (rear), of sufficient depth to enable the masker to wear it tightly secured in a horizontal position atop his head. The rear sides of most Koranko masks are flat, enabling them to be worn flush with the masker's torso.

This can easily be appreciated by comparing the above-described Koranko masks with four Toma masks from Macenta, Guinea.

The anthropozoomorphic Toma *Buzogi* mask (elsewhere called *Okobuzogui*[24]) in Figure 9 is an exquisite example of the style. It has inward-curling horns of the ram that must be sacrificed to it, and a non-articulated, heavily toothed jaw of a crocodile. Behind the top half of the mask, above the lower jaw, is a hollow space several inches deep, into which the wearer inserts the top of his head. The mask can then be tied under the masker's chin snugly enough so that it doesn't shift position while he dances. A ring of tightly rolled cloth placed inside the mask helps to add stability and comfort.

Figure 9. Toma *Buzogi* Horizontal Mask.
Macenta, Guinea
Height 25 inches (64 cm).
Wood, cowry shells, metal, animal hair and sacrificial material.
Private collection.
With its ram's horns and crocodile's jaws, the planar face on this large and heavy mask is unmistakably Toma in style. Like most Toma masks, it is worn horizontally, tied snugly on the wearer's head. (Photograph by N. Carey).

Figure 10. A Poro *Zo* demonstrating how the Toma *Buzogi* mask is worn horizontally atop his head. He would never have allowed his hands and legs to be seen if this had been a genuine masquerade. (In: Gaisseau 1954, Fig. 19).

The Toma in the area of Macenta, in the hinterland between Guinea and Liberia, do not usually make *Bakorogi* masks, as the Loma do, carving instead the large flat *Angbai* masks. Like many Poro masks, the *Angbai* in Figure 9 functions both publicly in the village and secretly in the Bush. It acts as the liaison between the Poro Sacred Bush and the village. The aluminum applications on the forehead, temples and brow represent the same thing as white pigment means in many other regions: this Bush Spirit is the bringer of happy news.[38] After an initiatory cycle, animal blood is poured on the *Angbai* as a sacrifice. The three horns on the head have a double meaning. To the initiated Poro men (*keh nanu* in Loma) it shows that the mask is owned by an Elder in Poro, but to the non-initiated ("sinners", or *kpolo wai*) it indicates that the mask is a middleman, the two outside horns representing the Poro and the people, while the central spike represents the mask.[39]

Figure 11. A Toma *Angbai* mask from the Elders' Poro.
Macenta, Guinea
Wood, aluminum, fiber, fabric.
Before 1920
Height 23 inches
Private collection. (Photograph by N. Carey).

The ancient Toma *Angbai* mask in Figure 12 is from the same Macenta region of Guinea as the previous one. This example is very old, dating from the third quarter of the nineteenth century or earlier, and is in the oldest known Macenta style.

The metal eyes show the power of the mask in its ability to control the people. The three horns refer to all three levels of Poro, as this mask is used in all Poro levels. Toma masks with only two horns from the

Macenta area are for the Men's initiation. Other masks with two quarter-circles facing outwards and a single fishtail in the center are Boys' Poro masks from this region, as the fishtail refers to the river where the circumcisions are performed in front of the all-powerful water spirit. [41]

The *Angbai* is not a singing mask (if it were, it would have an articulated jaw); it can see but not talk. It shares a similar function to the *Mã Da Ba* mask that collects the young boys when a new Bush session opens, but it collects the men for the Men's Poro. Of course, there is no need to collect old men for the Elders' Poro, as they are "already in possession of a strong enough Poro soul".

It is not within the scope of this work to elaborate upon the many different styles of Loma masks, nor to unduly discuss their functions within the Poro.[32] This image is included here mainly to demonstrate the magnitude of the front-to-back hollowness of the mask, in order to illustrate a structural distinction from the Koranko body masks. Although it certainly does not approach the deep bowl-like structure of a helmet mask, it nevertheless has sufficient rear concavity to enable it to be worn atop the head (usually lying on a ring of rolled cloth for comfort).

Figure 12. A Toma *Angbai* horizontal mask.
Macenta, Guinea.
Wood with metal
3rd quarter of the 19th century or earlier.
Height 21 inches (53 cm).
Private collection.
This ancient Toma *Angbai* mask is in the oldest known Macenta style. The three horns refer to all three levels of Poro, and this mask is used in rituals of all three levels. In contrast to Koranko masks, the deep hollowed back of this mask facilitates its being worn horizontally atop the head. (Photograph by Dr. N. Carey).

The enormous Toma *Landai*, like the *Buzogi*, is a terrifying (at least to the young boys) anthropozoomorphic mask combining carved horns on the head with the elongated, many-toothed jaws of a crocodile (Figure 11). It is the Bush Spirit that symbolically "eats" the young Poro initiates upon their initial entry into the Sacred Bush to begin their long period of training, after which time they are given new names, and are considered members of the community, distinct from women and uninitiated males. Although it is a powerful mask of the Elders' Poro, it is seen publicly. Like the *Angbai* and the *Buzogi* masks, it is worn balanced horizontally on the head. Because of its great length and weight, the wearer needs to support its snout with his hands, as illustrated in Figure 13. The protruding, rounded forehead creates an underlying bowl-shaped space into which the wearer places the top of his head (Figure 14). Attached strips of rolled cotton fabric are tied underneath his chin to secure the mask in place, and the entire head and body of the wearer is concealed underneath a full-length raffia costume. This *Landai* example, unusual in the high quality of its carving and in its unarticulated jaw, once wore a large headdress of long Great Blue Turaco feathers.

Figure 13. A Toma *Landai* Horizontal Mask.
Macenta, Guinea
Wood, animal hides, fabric, antelope horns, metal and accumulated sacrificial material.
Length 28 inches (71 cm)
Private collection.
Most Loma (Toma) masks are worn in a horizontal position balanced atop the head. The masquerader's entire body is hidden underneath a full-length raffia costume, as no part of the human may be seen (Harley 1941 p. 28). This is an unusually fine carving of a local variant of the *Landai*, which, although large and imposing, is usually rather roughly hewn.

Figure 14. Rear view of a Toma *Landai* mask.
The rear view of this Toma *Landai* mask reveals the deep bowl-shaped depression into which the wearer's head fits, and the cloth strips that are tied tightly underneath his chin to secure the mask firmly while it is being danced.

Figure 15. A Toma *Landai* mask in full costume.
The long, heavy mask is balanced horizontally atop the masquerader's head. (In: Eberl-Elber 1936, Fig. 195).

Figure 16. A Toma masquerader wearing *Landai* mask.

George Way Harley published this drawing, showing how a masquerader in costume supports the heavy snout of the horizontal Toma *Landai* mask with his hands (Harley 1941, p. 28).

At 10 inches in height, the small mask in Figure 17 can only be considered "miniature" in relation to the large Loma mask that it replicates. The *Zo* who owned and wore its larger brother carried this version with him when he attended sessions of the Elders' Poro within the Sacred Grove whenever important Poro matters were being discussed. Each Elder placed his miniature mask on a bed of special leaves, demonstrating his ownership of the large mask and his right to attend the meeting. This is not a "passport" mask *per se*, as it did not need to be shown in order to be admitted.

Stylistically this miniature mask is quite interesting. The most notable aspect is the addition of four strips of hammered aluminum, two slanting downward and inward on the cheeks, and two, mostly covered with old sacrificial material, slanting outward from the mouth downward to the chin. This places the mask into the small body of known Poro masks with aluminum strip ornamentation.[33] The use of aluminum strips and aluminum eyes indicates that this mask (and the large one) is used in the Boys' Poro rituals.

Figure 17. A Loma miniature mask.
Liberia/Guinea
Wood with aluminum, iron, fabric, power material and sacrificial material.
Height 10 inches (25 cm).
Private collection.
(Photograph by N. Carey)

The form itself is also fascinating. It is a splicing of two other Loma forms. From the nose upward, it is a very fine rendering of a Toma mask, with the gently curved horns and incised alternating diamond pattern seen on the most-powerful *Masgui* (Figure 8). From the nose downward, however, it is a *Bakorogi* mask, complete with the classical protruding triangular lips and pointed chin.[34] Its sides are decorated with the same incised pattern of alternating diamonds, instead of the more typical striations of the *Bakorogi*.

There are several aspects of this small mask indicating that whatever its particular function may have been, it was certainly an object of extreme power. There is a 5/8-inch (1.6 cm) wide, round hole in the top of the head between the two horns where some unknown object was once anchored, apparently tubular in cross section. This was certainly a medicine container. Inspection of the hole reveals the considerable thickness of encrusted, accumulated sacrificial applications over many generations. This is exactly the same spot on the head where the *Masgui* has its medicine pot containing blood and other powerful medicines.

The two horns on this mask are of characteristic Loma form, and have nothing do with indicating its Poro grade. Rather, it is the application of aluminum to the face that signifies the Boys' level. Had the metal strips been of brass, e.g., this would be an Elders' mask.

The encrusted top also holds the remains of several iron "Kissi pennies", as seen on only the most powerful Loma objects, such as the *Bakorogi* and the *Zo*'s medicine jar (Figure 18). A piece of iron rod is also present in the small mouth opening, and another piece can be seen protruding downward from the point of the chin. A packet of unknown power material, wrapped tightly in coarse native fabric, is tucked underneath the upper margin on the rear of the mask, affixed with more than twenty pieces of locally forged iron. Whereas aluminum, copper and brass are added to Poro sculpture as an indication of grade level (Boys', Men's, Elders'), iron, when added to Poro sculpture, both imparts and reveals great strength. Amongst the Kran, Kru, Bété and other Kruan-speaking groups to the south and east, iron is most commonly added in the form of upholstery tacks, often applied to masks in a symmetrical fashion. Amongst the northeastern Mande-speakers, particularly the Loma, Gbandi, Kpelle and even the adjacent but Kuwaa-speaking Belle, iron is usually applied in the form of rods or Kissi pennies (both of which are present on this example).

Figure 18 shows a rare and powerful Loma power object that belonged to a Poro *Zo*. In Loma it is called *Kwo Wale* (Big Doctor). It contains a powerful Spirit within its large terracotta jar, represented by the Janus-headed figural post rising from the sealed lid. It was kept in the home of the *Zo*, and was used specifically for healing the sick. People who came to visit the *Zo* would first make an offering to the medicine jar, and then get herbal or spiritual help. The figure is Janus-faced to represent the male and female nature of it, as well as its ability to see any bad magic that has been wished on someone.

Figure 18. *Kwo Wale,* **a Figural Urn of a Loma** *Zo.*
Zorzor, Liberia
Terracotta. White pigment, iron, unknown contents
Height 16 inches (40.5 cm).
Private collection

Made of terracotta, the upper half of the vessel is coated with kaolin (white clay). Protruding from the top of the head are several "Kissi pennies", small pieces of twisted iron flattened at the ends, once used as currency. These are only applied onto the most powerful and sacred Loma objects, and attest to their strength and value.

This object was collected in Zorzor near the Guinea border. Its rarity lies in the fact that its lid is still sealed, and its powerful medicinal contents, whatever they might be, are still contained within it, undisturbed. This is quite unusual, as these objects are rarely parted with, and certainly not with the terracotta bottom still containing a Spirit of Healing.

The two horns atop the head of each little mask-like face on either side of the figural stopper are classically Loma in style. They are not there to communicate grade or strength. That is done by the form itself, by the addition of the iron and by the addition of medicines.

An Enigma: The Stone Mask

Recently, a stone mask, carved entirely from a brownish steatite and weighing 10 pounds (4.5 kg)., drew the attention of the author (Figure 17). The history and function of this remarkable and possibly unique object are unknown. None of the author's Poro associates in Liberia or Guinea had ever seen or heard of one.

Stone was very rarely used in sub-Saharan African sculpture. Until recently, stone sculptures were reported from only limited areas: "…stone carving seems to have been practiced only in four places, though suitable stone is more generally available: in Sierra Leone and the neighboring Kissi area of Guinea, around Ife in Western Nigeria, on the upper Cross River near the Cameroon border of Eastern Nigeria; and on the south bank of the Congo…" (Fagg and Plass 1964, p. 18) [35]

The overall form appears to be in an archaic style from the Macenta area of Guinea, based on its thin, flat ovoid structure with the top cut horizontally, the thin brow band, its lack of a mouth, and its array of horns. The fact that it is made of stone is quite remarkable, however, as Loma stone carvings, though known, are extremely rare. Only about eight to ten have ever been published, and those examples were small figural objects similar to *nomoli* carvings (Van Damme 1991; Page 2005, p. 46-53; Tagliaferri 1989, 102-3, 129).

This is the only known large stone mask from this region [36]. Clearly, this mask was not meant to be worn, and accordingly it lacks holes for the attachment of a headdress, costume or body tethers. In speculating about the possible function of this mask, one can look to other Poro cultures for masks with similar characteristics, since different groups often share the same mask form for similar uses (although the same mask type can have completely different functions in neighboring groups).

One of the main commonalities of all Poro groups is the presence of a powerful Water Spirit who initiates and empowers the Poro among men; this relationship explains a chief reason for locating the Sacred Grove next to a river. The Gio (the Dan people living in Liberia) have a politically important all-metal mask that is not worn. When a strong Poro center desires to extend its sphere of influence to include a village without its own Poro, it places this heavy mask, called *Ku'Wo,* under water on the bottom of a river. When the mask is subsequently "found" by an initiate who "had a dream" about it, and then dove into the water and retrieved it, it is deemed due to the will of the great Water Spirit. A local chapter of Poro is thereby established, which is beholden to the older group. The fact that *Ku'wo* is made of heavy metal with a dull, non-reflective surface helps keep it submerged and unnoticed until it is retrieved. *Ku'wo* has a wooden agent mask, called *Ku'wo B'wou*, that precedes it and announces its coming.

The non-buoyancy and heavy weight of this stone mask would certainly ensure that it would stay hidden and immobile if placed on the bottom of a river. It might, therefore, be the equivalent of the correspondingly rare metal mask of the Gio. and serve a similar function. It may well be the founding Spirit of the Poro among its Poro group, and when "discovered" lying submerged in the river, it empowers the construction of a new Sacred Bush, and all of its descending hierarchy of Bush Spirit masks.

Another consideration is the durability of stone compared to wood in the hot and humid environment of the Guinea Coast. Insect pests, fungi and other microorganisms quickly damage wooden artifacts. Despite the best efforts at preservation, such as storing masks in the roof of a hut above a smokey fire, wooden objects simply don't last long in the African bush.

The most powerful and important masks in the Dan pantheon are made of metal, historically a valuable and rare commodity in the region.[40] The very fact that a mask has been created from metal or stone speaks volumes about the ritual value and importance of the work.

The age of this carving is unknown. Unlike wooden objects that have a short lifespan, stone may last for millennia. Although the Loma people migrated to the Guinea region from northern savannah areas about five hundred years ago, it is not inconceivable that this valuable Bush Spirit mask was brought along with them, since Poro pre-dated the migration of the Mande-speaking peoples. In fact, the very word "Loma" is Mandingo meaning to join to, to go into a secret society, to be initiated, and therefore implies the existence of the Poro before the ancient naming of the group itself.[37]

Figure 19. An ancient stone mask, probably Koranko.
Sierra Leone/Guinea/Liberia?
Steatite
Height 12.25 inches (31 cm)
Private collection
(Photograph by N. Carey)

For several years it was attributed to the Toma by its owner, a New England dealer in Asian art. The style of this mask poses an enigma, however. Although the overall form of the brow and face are mildly suggestive of the Toma, as is the form of the small horns, the number of horns is atypical. There are six horns, one of which broke off long ago. This multiplicity of horns is, as already noted, a stylistic trait of the Koranko, and is used to indicate a particularly high Poro grade level and strength. The shortness of the horns must be ignored. Steatite, also called soapstone, is relatively soft, and can easily be carved with the same tools used for woodcarving. Horns of any great length would surely break off; even with the short length on this carving, one horn has broken.

In addition, the carver took deliberate pains to deeply incise nostrils on the long but angled nose. Except for the *Bakarogi* masks of the Loma, which were adopted by the Loma from the neighboring Kpelle (called the Guerzé in Guinea), Loma masks' noses are straight, smooth, and seem to lack nostrils. Kpelle and Gbandi sculpted noses are angled and have nostrils like these.

The stone mask therefore possesses a conglomerate of stylistic traits that, for the past two centuries at least, have individually belonged to several Mande-speaking groups in eastern Sierra Leone, northeastern Liberia and Southeastern Guinea. If this mask was indeed sculpted in the last 200 years or thereabout, one could then say with some certainty that it is a Koranko mask exhibiting some Kpelle and Toma influence. But, in truth, its age is a mystery. If, as is very possible, it is more than half a millenium old, then it dates from the time before or during the Mande migrations to their present-day territories. It might in fact be a sort of Rosetta Stone, revealing several ancient styles fused together in one work of art, but otherwise lost in African prehistory.

A Revisitation of Published Examples

It is quite apparent that there are distinct and easily recognizable stylistic differences between Koranko and Toma masks, but it is also apparent why Koranko masks might be confused with those of the Toma by observers who are unfamiliar with this rare style. The same Loma or Toma attribution keeps reappearing in the ethnographic art literature, including catalogs of Museum collections and galleries, and in tribal art journals.[31]

Just where, when, or how the first Koranko-Loma mix-up began is not certain. One can imagine the scenario where, sometime within the past few centuries, a Koranko mask made its way to a Western observer who was somewhat familiar with the Toma style, but not with their lesser-known neighbors, and the misattribution was made. Perhaps a Koranko mask was collected somewhere in Sierra Leone, Guinea or Liberia, and was unknowingly attributed to the Toma/Loma. Nevertheless, the Koranko style is distinct from that of the Toma. If anything, it is in some ways more akin to some Temne Bush Spirit masks from the western part of their range, than to the Toma to their east (see Figure 7).

The Peabody Museum of Archaeology and Ethnology at Harvard University has in its collection a Koranko body mask[9] in perhaps its simplest form, labeled "Senufo; Toma" (Figure 20). It consists of no more than an elongated plank, 29 inches (74 cm) high, oval on the bottom (chin) and cut horizontally across the top. It sports two horns of round cross section atop the head, curving inward and almost meeting in the midline. Although there are multiple holes along its periphery, the wooden form is devoid of all its prior attachments and sacrificial materials. In this naked state, the mask might well serve as a template for all other Koranko Boys' Poro masks.

Figure 20. A Koranko Boys' Poro Mask in Harvard's Peabody Museum. Upon this simple wooden form, now missing all of its attachments and sacrificial remnants, an elaborate example of African accumulative sculpture once existed. However, it can still be identified as a Koranko mask from the Boys' level of Poro.

Figure 21 shows an image of a very simple, unadorned body mask from the Guggenheim collection. It was published in 1965 and again in 1966 as a Loma mask.[10] Quite similar to the Peabody example, it has been stripped of all its attachments except for its round mirror eyes (Figures 3 and 4 also have such eyes). The two horns indicate that it is from the Boys' Poro. Although it is clearly a Koranko mask, this particular example exhibits a great deal of Toma influence. Each horn is rather thick at the base, round in cross section and tapers gracefully, with significant space between the two. In addition, the long, straight nose without nostrils, extending downward from the overhanging brow, is a Toma stylistic feature. This is an example of the intermixture of styles so commonly seen amongst the sculpture of neighboring Poro groups.[11]

Figure 21. A Koranko Boys' Poro mask.
Height 35 inches (90 cm)
Wood, mirrors, native repair with fiber.
(P. Guggenheim collection, In: Fagg 1965, 1966).

Figure 22 shows another fascinating example of Toma influence on Koranko style in a mask that was attributed to the Toma.[26] This is a large (30 ½ inches, 77 cm), classical Elders' mask from the Koranko Poro . It is three-tiered like the example in Figure 5. The largest, bottom tier has four large, inwardly curving horns of round cross section. The middle tier has one large central horn, and the small top tier has two small horns and a cloth-covered medicine packet. The whole is encrusted with sacrificial material.

What makes this mask so very intriguing is the shallow concavity on the back. This is revealed in the photograph by the peripheral attachment holes, which are along the sides of the mask and not bored from front to back as on a simple plank mask. The same features are found on the Elders' mask in Figure 5. The reason for this stylistic difference between the Elders' masks and the masks of the lower levels is unknown to this author.

Figure 22. A Koranko Elders' Poro Mask.

Height 30 ½ inches (77 cm). Wood, fabric, medicine packet containing power materials, sacrificial residue. Similar in form to the *Elders'* mask in Figure 6, it has round horns on three tiers, a flared snout, a medicine packet and a shallowly concave back.

Another two Koranko masks were attributed to the Loma in journal article.[27] The first one is from the Men's level of Poro (Figure 23). It is plank-like in form, 33 ½ inches (85 cm) high, and sports seven horns atop its head, all extending from one tier. There is one small central horn flanked by a pair of longer straight horns on each side, and on the outside by a larger pair of inwardly curving horns of square cross section. On the forehead is a red (the color of Poro) fabric-covered medicine packet. It has a small, straight nose, a short, solid, beard-like snout carved under the chin, and a shallowly incised mouth similar to that seen in Figure 4. The authors erroneously call this a horizontal mask.

Figure 24 shows the second one, a relatively small (19 inches, 48 cm), even less refined body mask from the Boys' Poro. Its two horns are angled inward, rather than curved, and have a rectangular cross section. Multiple attachments obscure the mask below the brow. In addition to raffia, there is an attached antelope horn containing an unknown concoction of medicine and wrapped in cloth, as well as beads and coins from Liberia and French West Africa dating from the 1940's.

Figure 23. A Koranko mask from the Men's Poro.
Height 33 ½ inches (85 cm)
Wood, cowry shells, red fabric-covered medicine pouch.
Collection of the Africana Museum, Cuttington University College, Gbarnga, Liberia.
This mask from the Men's level of Poro has square-based horns, and displays the beveled edge seen in Figure 4.

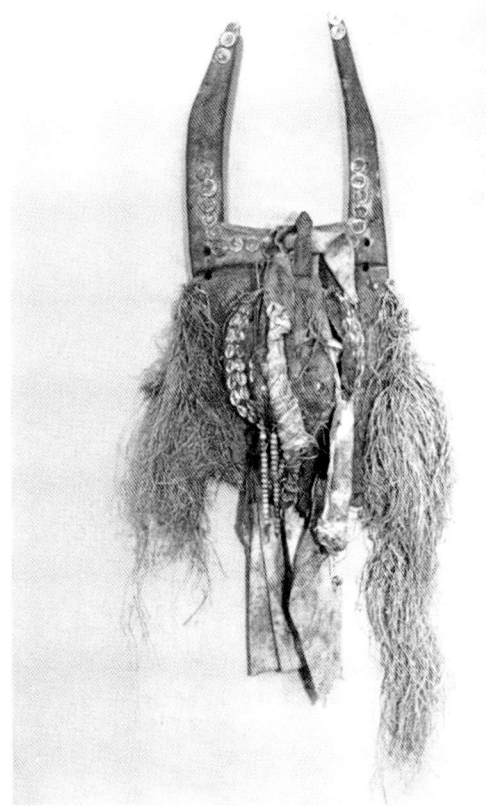

Figure 24. A Koranko Boys' Poro Body Mask.
Height 19 inches (48 cm)
Wood, cowry shells, cloth and cowry shell medicine packet, antelope medicine horn wrapped in white cloth, beads, Liberian and French West African coins from the 1940's.
Collection of the Africana Museum, Cuttington University College, Gbarnga, Liberia.

Figure 25 shows a five-horned Men's Poro body mask in the same substyle as the former two masks: the cross section of the horns are rectangular. Two animal horns from the indigenous spiral-horned antelope, the harnessed bushbuck, protrude from the top of the medicine packet. Beads and cowry shells adorn the mask and encrusted sacrificial material coats the entire piece. This mask was attributed to the Loma in an exhibition catalogue.[28]

Figure 25. A five-horned Koranko mask from the Men's Poro.
Height 29 inches (74 cm)
Wood, fabric, horns, cowries, beads, medicine packet.
(In: Kahan, 1979).

In her 1987 manuscript, Van Damme included a fascinating old Koranko body mask from the Boys' level of Poro, which she labeled a "*Nyangbai*" mask (Figures 11 and 12 are Toma *Angbai* masks). Viewed from the front, it has two curved horns with square bases, and a simple midline nose of triangular cross section extending down from the protruding horizontal brow. The empty space between the horns, from the brow line upward, is filled with a large cloth-wrapped medicine packet (Figure 26).

From the rear, however, one is able to see what appears to be a smaller third horn, sticking straight up from the midline between the two curved outer horns, and obscured from the front view by the large medicine packet. This is very reminiscent of the middle horns found on the masks in Figures 3 and 4. In addition, it shares the bevel around the edge of the face, through which the attachment holes are bored, seen in Figure 4. The overall flat plank-like form shows no evidence of rear concavity.

Figure 26. A Koranko Boys' Poro body mask. Height 28 inches (72 cm). Wood, animal hides, fabric, leather, metal, cowry shells, horns and diverse attachments. Collection S. Du Chastel. Watermaal-Bosvoorde, Belgium. Similar to the masks in Figures 3 and 4, this plank mask from the Boy's Poro appears to have a straight central horn, visible only from the rear. It shares the same facial beveling as the Men's mask in Figure 4. (In: Van Damme 1987).

Figure 27 shows a Koranko body mask in the collection of the Indiana University Art Museum, used as an example of a Loma horizontal mask in a journal article entitled "Is There History in Horizontal Masks?"[12] It is from the Boy's level of Poro, 38 inches (96.5 cm) in height, with two rounded horns and a cloth and fiber-covered medicine packet.

45

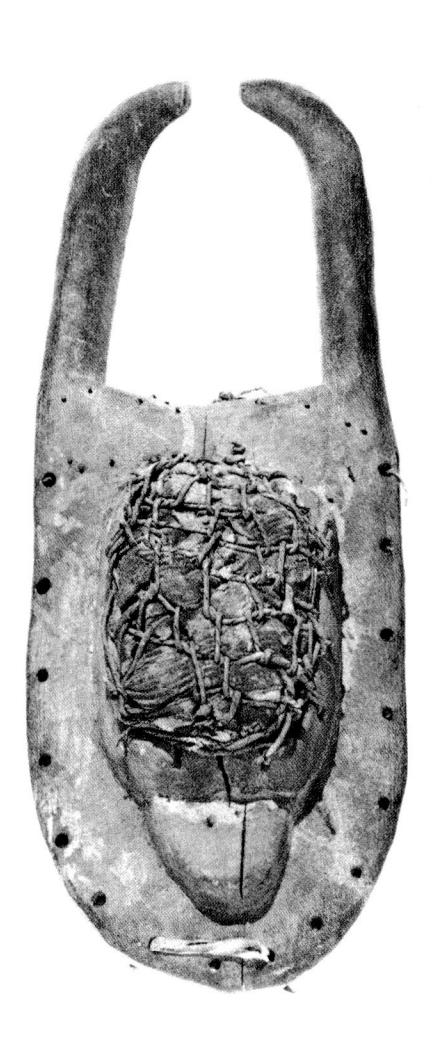

Figure 27. A Koranko Boys' Poro body mask.
Height 38 inches (96.5 cm).
Wood, fiber, fabric, power material.
(Indiana University Art Museum Number 63.238).

The M. H. de Young Memorial Museum in San Francisco has in its collection[13] a Boys' Poro mask with two long, finely carved horns of round cross section (Figure 28). Raffia is attached using its peripheral holes, beads and cloth are applied, and a medicine horn is suspended from mid-forehead.

Figure 28. A Koranko Boys' Poro body mask.
Height 34 inch (86.4 cm)
Wood, metal, fiber, beads, fabric, power materials.
(Photograph: M. H. de Young Memorial Museum, San Francisco).

Figure 29 shows a typical five-horned mask from the Koranko Men's Poro, similar in form to the mask in Figure 3. It is currently in a New York collection, and was recently offered for sale as a Toma mask. It is classical in style, with its five horns of round cross section, cloth covered medicine packet adorned with cowry shells, dangling medicine horn and plank-like form. It has a small, elongated nose without nostrils.

Figure 29. A Koranko Men's Poro body mask.
Wood, red fabric, medicine packet, cowry shells, fiber, animal horn filled with power material, sacrificial residue.
Height 22 inches (56 cm)
Private collection.

Figure 30 shows an important and exquisite example of a Koranko body mask from the Men's Poro. It was offered as Lot 121 in the Zemanek Tribal Art Auction catalogue of May 2007, where it was described as a Toma zoomorphic mask. In addition to the characteristic five horns, finely rendered by a master carver, it sports a very well made and symmetrically composed medicine packet with a circle of cowrie shells surrounding a central glass mirror. As previously noted, mirrored glass is a powerful medicine when attached to masks of the Loma and the Koranko, and is present on the masks in Figures 3, 4 and 6. The incised mouth and small straight nose are typical, but of interest is the incised diamond pattern along the periphery of the face.

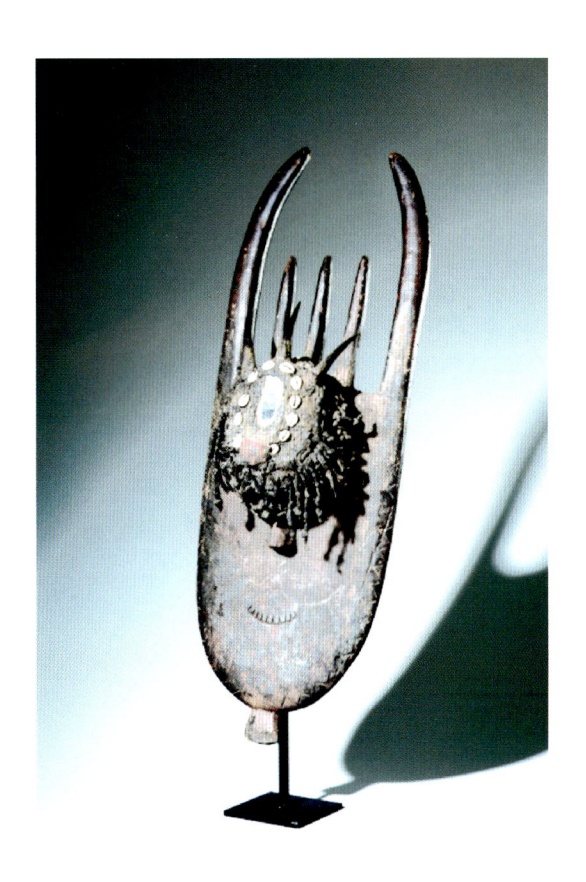

Figure 30. A Koranko Men's Poro body mask.
Wood, medicine packet with cowry shells, red fabric, mirrored glass, and three antelope horns, filled with unknown power material, sacrificial residue.
Height: 40 1/4 inches (102.5 cm)
Private collection. (In: Zemanek-Münster 2007. Photograph Eye-D Photodesign, Nürnberg).

Stylistic Variations

It is apparent that there are stylistic variations within this corpus of Koranko masks that are not well understood. Although the overall forms remain the same, subtle differences amongst the lot separate them into two distinct groups.

The first group, consisting of those masks in Figures 3, 4, 6, 20, 21, 22, 27, 28, and 29 are more finely sculpted. The horns in particular are carefully and gently tapered toward their tips, and are round in cross section from their bases to their points. The outer horns curve gracefully upward and toward the midline. The second group of masks, as noted in Figures 23-26, possesses horns that are rectangular in cross section, retaining the squared edges that were produced after the carver first created the horns by excising the wood between them from the simple blank wooden plank from which he produced the mask, with only some minimal smoothing of the sharp edges. Additionally, the inward curvature of the horns is less graceful and more angular, the horns often tapering only partially in a coarse fashion.

The key to these stylistic differences might be found by starting with a known factor —location. Unfortunately, collection notes are lacking from previously published examples. However, we do know that the set of three masks presented in the beginning of this work was collected from the hinterland where Koranko territory abuts that of the Toma in Guinea. This is a very small area in the extreme southeastern tail of Koranko country.

Horns, when present on Toma masks, are generally smooth, gently tapered, gracefully curved, and round in cross section. These traits are apparent in the Loma carvings in Figures, 8, 11, 12, 13, 17, and 18.

As noted, Figure 22 shows a Koranko Elders' mask with strong Toma stylistic influence. Its horns, like the horns of masks in Figures 3, 5 and 6, share these same Toma features. These four Koranko masks all demonstrate the meticulously carved, smooth, round, thickly based, gently tapered and gracefully curved horns of the Toma, as do all of the nine masks in the first group.

It is therefore quite reasonable to surmise that Koranko masks originating in southeastern Guinea near Toma territory reveal strong Toma influence on their sculptural style, and can be distinguished from those Koranko masks originating from deeper into their territory in Guinea and Sierra Leone by the form of their horns. Horns with rounded cross sections, carefully tapering towards their tips, and gently curving inward indicate a southeastern Koranko style. Horns with a rectangular cross section, coarser tapering and an angular inward curvature are most likely of a more central and western origin. Certainly, more research is indicated to further elucidate this finding.

Summary

Different Poro groups throughout West Africa use different masking styles in order to communicate to observers the specific identity and status of each masked Bush Spirit. The Loma (called the Toma in Guinea), like the Dan, Mano, Kono, Kpelle and Belle, use the actual *form* of a mask, coupled with the application of specific added materials, to show its grade and strength. The Koranko, on the other hand, indicate increasing grade level and strength by adding to the actual *number of horns* carved on each mask, augmented by the addition of power materials. The most significant difference between the masks of the Koranko and most masks from the neighboring Toma lies in their manner of usage. Most Koranko masks are *body masks*, having flat undersides, which facilitates their being worn flush against the back of the masquerader's torso (the Elders' mask, which is not worn, is an exception). Most Toma masks are *horizontal masks*, having hollowed undersides that facilitate snug attachment on top of the masquerader's head. Because of superficial similarities between Koranko and Toma masks, the former have historically been prone to being attributed to the Toma.

Notes

1. For a detailed analysis of the traditional and contemporary use of secrecy by the Poro in maintaining political power, see Tefft (1992).

2. Bordogna (1988) states that in addition to the Loma, the Gbandi and Kissi also produce large horizontal masks. Unfortunately, he did not document this further. Celenko (1983: 64) published a photograph by William Siegmann, taken in 1973, showing a *Landai* masker in full costume resting in the village of Bolahun in Kissi territory of Northeastern Liberia. According to Celenko, Siegmann thought the *Landai* mask (See Figure 9 below) originated with the Gbandi (who live between the Kissi and Loma in Liberia). Benjamin Dennis, himself a Gbandi, noted that the Gbandi have both the horizontally worn *Landai* and *Angbai* masks (1972).

3. The actual performance of the circumcision ritual holds varying degrees of importance among different Poro groups, but universally a boy must be circumcised before he can be initiated into Boys' Poro. In the case of the Koranko, the *birike* (circumcision ritual) is conducted in a separately constructed Circumcision Bush (*biri* or *bili*) during a period of about three weeks during the dry season (McCulloch 1950: 92).

4. For insight into Kpelle Poro secrecy, see Bellman (1984) and Tefft (1992). See Glaze (1981) regarding Senufo Poro secrecy. Carey (2008) extensively analyzes the art and rituals of most known Poro groups.

5. The translation of the Koranko word *Gah'* is unknown at this time. The nearby Mano, who are Mande speakers like the Koranko, have the word *ga*, meaning "to die, dead, death". *Ga mia*, for example, a term for human spirits, literally means "dead people" (Schwab 1947: 493-494). If the term *Gah* is related to the Mano *ga*, one might connect the masks to the ritual symbolic death and rebirth of the boys when they first enter Boys' Poro, when they are "eaten" by a powerful and frightening masked Bush Spirit, given a new name, and "reborn" as a member of Poro. Both the Mano and the Dan use the word *Ga* (pronounced Gaw) for God (Schwab, 1947 p. 498), but this is an unlikely association, as the local concept of God is one of an aloof celestial entity, whereas masks are corporeal Bush Spirits living on Earth. The Dan also use the word *ga* for a leopard (*ga gɛ* is the mask of the "Leopard Devil"), but this seems unrelated. Nasalized, the Dan word *ga* means "male". The Mano use the term *ga geh* for the "Big Devil", a powerful judgment mask equivalent to the *Nyamu* in other groups (Schwab 1947: 269; Harley 1950: 11). In the nearby Guerzé tongue (the Kpelle in Guinea) the word *Gã* equals *ka*, "to engender" (Casthelain 1952:136 and 180), or *Kã*, a basket for carrying on the head (183). The latter seems ironically inappropriate for a body mask. The Dan have a well-known mask that is publicly displayed called *Gagon* or *Ga Gon*, usually translated as "frisky Bush Devil". In this case, *Ga* is the equivalent of *Gɛ*, the generic Dan name for all Bush Spirits or

"Devils" and their masks. Fischer also equates *Gä* to the more usual Gɛ (Fischer 1978: 19). These refer to anthropozoomorphic bird-like bearded masks that are stylistically quite dissimilar to those of the Koranko and Loma, although they may share some similar functions. Schwab notes the use of *Mã* as a generic term for mask in Gbandi, Loma and Mano It is felt at this point that these "*Gah'* "masks are all *Nyenne* (Bush Spirit) masks from the Koranko Poro, and the word *Gah'* is probably equivalent to *Nyenne, Gɛ and Ga.*

6. McCulloch (1950: 92) uses the name *Gbangbami* for the Poro of the Koranko. Jackson (1977: 34-35, 225) applies the term *Gbangbe* to the association, *Gbongbone* to the name of the *Zo* (medicine man, shaman, priest) and *Komebon* to the Sacred Bush. *Gbangbe* has "more secretiveness and seriousness" [than other spirits/cults, like *Kome*], and never has public displays. This suggests a parallel between *Gbangbe* and the more powerful masked Bush Spirits in Elders' Poro. Ayittey (2006) also uses *Gbangbe, while* McCullough cites Thomas' (1916) use of *Andoma.*

7. The author is indebted to his associate M. S. Aboudoulaye, himself a Poro initiate, for details regarding Koranko and Loma masking traditions (Aboudoulaye 1999).

8. Scarification among the groups in this area is of two types, cosmetic and cult-related. Most ritual scarification in the region is performed by the Loma (Toma), Kissi, Gbandi and Kpelle, all of them in very close proximity to the Koranko. Figure 4 illustrates some body and limb scarification patterns of the Loma, Gbandi and Kissi Men's and Boys' Poro. (Schwab 1947: 118-119; Germann 1933:20-23).

9. Peabody Number 973-25-50/11646.

10. Fagg 1965, plate 9 and 1966, plate 3.

11. For an extensive treatment of the intermixture of styles in Poro art, refer to Carey 2008.

12. Indiana University Art Museum Number 63.238. In: McNaughton 1991, p. 51 fig. 20.

13. In his book *Indigenous African Institutions*, George Ayittey notes that the Poro of the Vai people is called *Beri*, while that of the Koranko is the *Gbangbe*, and that of the Kpaa Mende is the *Wunde* (*Wonde* in Abraham, 1978 p. 25). He states that the Poro associations of the Mende, Kono, Temne, Vai, Limba and Koranko are "all practically identical in their organization and function."

14. *Kome* is the name of both the association and "a powerful and dangerous bush spirit" (Jackson, 1977 p. 34-35, 225). Jackson speaks of the *Kome* and the *Gbangbe* as two separate cult associations. However, he seems to be describing the same organizational structure and function as other Poro groups, wherein different *Zoes* specialize in different skills, and the hierarchy is based on age levels, possession of esoteric knowledge, and relative strength of medicines. In this case, *Kome* appears to be a specific Bush Spirit who

enforces social control through the administration of potent biological and chemical agents (of which Jackson knew of three types) and through knowledge and control of antidotes. *Gbangbe* has "more secretiveness and seriousness", and unlike the *Kome*, it never has public displays. This suggests a parallel between the *Gbangbe* and those more powerful masked Bush Spirits in other Poro groups, which are seen only within the confines of the Sacred Bush, and sometimes only by the Elders' Poro. As Jackson never saw, nor was informed of, any masking tradition associated with these associations, he concluded that "carved masks are unknown among the Kuranko" (p. 236 note 23). Elsewhere, Jackson describes sacrifices to *Kome*. He describes a chicken being sacrificed by *Kome* cult members for soliciting the Bush Spirit's protection against witchcraft, sorcery or enemies. Apparently the chicken is thrown on the ground "in the direction of the cult object (symbolizing the spirit)", but unfortunately Jackson does not describe the object. This is most likely a mask or figure (Jackson 1977b p. 128.

15. McCulloch, 1950 p. 92 cites Luke, J. F., 1939. *Some Impressions of the Koranko and their Country.* Sierra Leone Studies, XXII.

16. Fairhead and Leach (1996) report that Bush Spirits of the neighboring Kissi, a Mel-speaking group, are called *ŋina*, a term also used also by the Koranko (elsewhere called *Nyenne* (pp 90-92). Poro variants closer to the Komo (Komé) of the Koranko are practiced among the more northern Kissi (p. 111).

17. Schwab (1947) uses the term *Poro* (p. 266) for the Mano association, which they originally adopted from the Kpelle, the term meaning "to cut" or "a cutting", referring to the circumcision ritual.

18. According to oral history, the Loma originally learned about Poro from the Kissi. The very name "Loma" is a Manding word meaning to join to, to go into a secret society, to be initiated. Hence, Poro members are called *Loma-Mowly*, meaning "the initiates" (Korvah, 1995 p. 19). It is said that the Poro is "older than the oldest tribe in Liberia" (Korvah p. 91).

19. According to Schwab, the full name of Gbandi Poro is *Polo gi zu*, meaning "Poro thing in", i.e., "in the Poro Society" (p. 267). He reports that the term *Polo* is also used by the Loma, whereas Leopold uses the term *Pölögii* (1991, 1996 p. 18).

20. According to Korvah, himself a Loma Poro initiate, *Dazoe* is the term for the Elder who is the highest officer of the Poro (1995 p. 91).

21. Dennis, 1972 p. 15.

22. Leopold, 1996 p. 27.

23. Hojbjerg (1999 p. 549, 550) uses *Kolou Zowoi* for the leader of the Loma Poro, the head *Zo*.

24. Gaisseau, a French documentary filmmaker, in 1954 traveled to Guinea and reported on a specific village's "Okobuzogui" mask. This was the name of only this village's Buzogi mask, referring to Oko, the community's ancestral founder, but has erroneously been used in the literature to refer to other Buzogi masks.

25. McCulloch, 1950 p. 92 cites Thomas, N. W., 1916. *Anthropological Report on Sierra Leone, Pt. 1.* Harrison and Sons, London.

Butt-Thompson wrote that the *Ampora*, the Poro of the Mende, historically split off from the Poro in order to preserve the "purity of the ancient ritual". Ampora then went on to influence the Koranko through *Andomba*, the Limba through *Banban*, the Lokko through *Dubaia*, and the Sherbro through *Torma* (1929 p. 241).

Butt-Thompson also mentions the *Andomba* while discussing the graphic signs of West African secret societies (170-173). He wrote: "Each society has one particular sign that may be used by all its members. These are invincible as protective agencies. Their presence is as sufficient as that of the highest official, indeed, of all the officials. It has supreme authority. 'A sure way of gaining redress, whether vengeance or the collecting of a debt, is to send the society sign.' Placed against the entrance to a village it is the most formidable tabu known, a prohibition against, say, trespass or theft, more formidable than any police, African or European." The sign of the *Ampora*, which influenced the *Andomba*, is a half-burned leaf. The sign of the Andomba is four triangles joined at right angles at their apices to form a cross:

26. Rubin 1974 p. 23 Fig. 17.

27. Siegmann and Schmidt 1977, p. 15. From the Cuttington University College Africana Museum.

28. Kahan 1979, p. 28.

29. See Jackson 1977 p.182 for a field photograph of young Koranko boys wearing these caps.

30. Van Damme (1987, Afb. 12, p. 12).

31. Propagation of printed misinformation is rife in the field of African art, and is often due to a simple, though well-intentioned, lapse of scholarship.

There also exists deliberate misattribution. An associate, currently in charge of the African and Oceanic Department at a major international auction house, once explained this. For example, it is often simply *easier* to label an object with the more familiar "Dan" moniker than it is to use the more correct Kpelle, Mano or Kono attribution. It is more difficult, and confusing to most readers, to try to explain the reasoning behind the correct attribution. In our case, it would be easier to attribute a mask to the better-known "wastebasket" group, the "Toma", than to the Koranko, Gbandi, Belle or some other less familiar group.

32. For an in-depth analysis of Loma art, refer to the large work *Poro, Power and Poison: Art of the West African Secret Society* (Carey 2008).

33. Hart (1987) describes a group of masks with metal strip ornamentation, mostly from Sierra Leone. Carey (2008) refers to the Loma *Mã Da Ba* mask of the Boys' Poro, and describes the use of metals by Poro groups as an indicator of grade level (2007b).

34. The *Bakorogi* is a distinctive class of Loma masks characterized by a protruding forehead overhanging a markedly geometrical face, a combination of triangular planes and diagonals that visually sets these masks apart from the more familiar elongated planar Loma face. The Loma originally got the Bakorogi from the neighboring Kpelle. For an exposition of the *Bakorogi* mask, see Carey 2008).

35. See also Allison, 1968 p. 7.

36. The author is familiar with two miniature stone masks from the Loma, previously unpublished.

37. Van Damme, 1991; Korvah, 1995 p. 19; O'Toole, 1995 p. 156.

38. When applied to a Poro mask, the color white, be it paint, kaolin or aluminum, often signifies that the mask brings happiness and good tidings. Thus, aluminum does not always indicate the Boys' grade level.

39. Schwab, 1947 pp. 268, 501, 503.

40. The most powerful object of the Dan Poro is an all-brass mask. Only three or four examples were ever known to exist, and one of those, seen by Talibi Kaba in the 1950's, was melted down when the Paramount Chief became a Christian, as this was considered the most sacred/evil piece of magic in the village. Although it has the classical form of a Gio mask, and even has attachment holes, it is not worn. This mask is the only object that represents the actual face of the Spirit of the Waters, the River God himself. It is the bearer of the brass medicine pot that is used to collect the ritual blood from the female circumcisions of the Sande, and then is brought back to the Elders to use as the grand Medicine container. (See Carey 2007b and 2008).

41. Parrinder expounds upon the widespread African belief in powerful, sacred water gods (1954 p. 49). However, this is taken to an extreme in Poro, where all power – to mask, to govern, to judge – flows from the great Water Spirit.

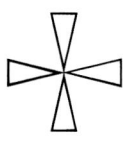

References

Aboudoulaye, M. S. 1999-2002. Personal Communications.

Abraham, A. 1978. Mende *Government and Politics under Colonial Rule: A Historical Study of Political Change in Sierra Leone, 1890-1937.* Sierra Leone U. P.: Freetown.

Allison, P. 1968. *African Stone Sculpture.* Lund Humphries: London

Ayittey, G. B. N. 2006. *Indigenous African Institutions.* Leiden, Hotei.

Bellman, B. L. 1984. *The Language of Secrecy: Symbols and Metaphors in Poro Ritual.* Rutgers University Press: New Brunswick, NJ.

Bordogna, C. 1988. *The Masks of Liberia: Appreciating a Heritage.* S.M.A. Museum: Tenafly, NJ.

Butt-Thompson, F. W. 1929. West African Secret Societies: Their Organisations, Officials and Teaching. H. F. G. Witherby: London.

Carey, N. 2007a. *Comparative Native Terminology of Poro Groups.* Ethnos Publications: Amherst, MA.

Carey, N. 2007b. *Making the Grade: The Meaning of Metals in Poro Art of West Africa.* Ethnos Publications: Amherst, MA.

Carey, N. 2008. *Poro, Power and Poison: Understanding the West African Secret Society through Art.* Ethnos Publications: Amherst, MA.

Casthelain, R. P. J. 1952. *La Langue Guerzé. In: Mémoires de l'Institut Français, No. 20.* IFAN: Dakar.

Celenko, T. 1983. *A Treasury of African Art from the Harrison Eiteljorg Collection.* Indiana University Press: Bloomington, IN.

Dennis, B. 1972. *The Gbandes: A People of the Liberian Hinterlands.* Nelson-Hall: Chicago.

Eberl-Elber, R. 1936. *Westafrikas Letztes Rätsel: Erlebnisbericht uber die Forschungsreise 1935 durch Sierra Leone.* Das Bergland-Buch: Salzburg.

Fairhead, J. and M. Leach (1996). *Misreading the African Landscape: Society and Ecology in a Forest-Savanna Mosaic*. Cambridge University Press: Cambridge.

Fagg, W. 1965. *Tribes and Forms in African Art*. Methuen, London.

Fagg, W. 1966. *African Tribal Sculptures: I. The Niger Basin Tribes*. Tudor Publishing: New York.

Fagg, W. and Plass, M. 1964. *African Sculpture; an Anthology*. London.

Fischer, E. 1978. *Dan Forest Spirits: Masks in Dan Villages*. African Arts XI, 2: 16-23. UCLA: Los Angeles.

Fischer, E. and Himmelheber, H. 1984. *The Arts of the Dan in West Africa*. Museum Rietberg: Zurich.

Foray, 1977. C. P. *Historical Dictionary of Sierra Leone*. (*African Historical Dictionaries, Volume 12*). Scarecrow Press: Metuchen, New Jersey.

Gaisseau, P-D. 1954. *The Sacred Forest: The Fetishist and Magic Rites of the Toma*. Weidenfeld & Nicholson: London.

Germann, P. 1933. *Die Völkerstämme im Norden von Liberia*. R. Voigtländers Verlag: Leipzig.

Glaze, A. J. 1981. *Art and Death in a Senufo Village*. Indiana University Press: Bloomington.

Gordon, Raymond G., Jr. (ed.), 2005. *Ethnologue: Languages of the World, Fifteenth edition*. Dallas, Tex.: SIL International. Online version: http://www.ethnologue.com/.

Harley, G. W. 1941. *Notes on the Poro of Liberia*.: Peabody Museum, Harvard: Cambridge, MA.

Harley, G. W. 1950. *Masks as Agents of Social Control in Northeast Liberia*. Peabody Museum, Harvard: Cambridge, MA.

Jackson, M. 1974. *The Structure and Significance of Kuranko Clanship, in Africa: Journal of the International African Institute*, 44:4 pp. 397-415.

Jackson, M. 1977a. *The Kuranko: Dimensions of Social Reality in a West African Society*. St. Martin's Press: New York.

Jackson, M. 1977b. *Sacrifice and Social Structure among the Kuranko. Part III: Sacrifice and Social Structure*. Africa: Journal of the International African Institute, 47, 2: 123-139.

Johnson, S. Jangaba M. 1974. *The Influence of Islam on Poro and Sande in Western Liberia. In: Seminar on African Studies, July 18-19, 1974*. University of Liberia: Monrovia.

Kahan Gallery.1979. *African Art of the West Atlantic Coast: Transition in Form and Content. Essay by Frederick Lamp*. Kahan Gallery: New York.

Korvah, P. 1995. *The History of the Loma People*. Oakland, O Books: CA.

McCulloch, M. 1950. *The Peoples of Sierra Leone. Ethnographic Survey of Africa, Western Africa, Part II*. Edited by D. Forde. International African Institute: London.

McNaughton, P. R. 1991. *Is there History in Horizontal Masks?* African Arts 24,2: 40-53.

Migeod, F. W. H.; Johnston, H. (1915). *Notes on West Africa According to Ptolemy*. Journal of the Royal African Society, 14(56), 414-426.

Migeod, F. W. H. 1916. *The Building of the Poro House*. Man XVI.

Olson, J. S. 1996. *The Peoples of Africa: An Ethnohistorical Dictionary*. Greenwood Press: Westport, CT.

O'Toole, T. E. 1995. *Historical Dictionary of Guinea*. (African Historical Dictionaries, Volume 16). Scarecrow Press: Lanham, MD .

Page, D. 2005. *Artists and Patrons in Traditional African Cultures: African Sculpture from the Gary Schulze Collection*. Queensborough Community College, CUNY: New York

Parrinder, G. 1954. *African Traditional Religion*. Greenwood Press: Westport, CT.

Paulme, D. 1954. *Les Gens du Riz. Kissi de Haute-Guinée Française*. Librairie Plon: Paris.

Rubin, A. 1974. *African Accumulative Sculpture*. Pace Gallery: New York.

Schwab, G. 1947. *Tribes of the Liberian Hinterland. Edited with Additional Material by George W. Harley*. Peabody Museum: Cambridge, MA.

Siegmann, W. C. and Schmidt, C. 1977. *Rock of the Ancestors: Namôa Koni.* Cuttington University College: Suakoko, Liberia.

Tagliaferri, A. 1989. *Stili del Potere: Antiche sculture in Pietra dalla Sierra Leone e dalla Guinea.* Electa: Milano.

Tefft, S. K. 1992. *The Dialectics of Secret Society Power in States.* Humanities Press: Atlantic Highlands, NJ.

Van Damme, A. 1987. *De Maskersculptuur Binnen het Poro-Genootscap van de Loma: Getuigenis van een Ecologisch-Culturelle Anpassing? (Poro-masks among the Loma. Witness of an ecological-cultural adaptation?) Working Papers in Ethnic Art.* State University of Ghent: Ghent.

Van Damme, A. 1991. *À Propos de Huit Sculptures en Pierre Découvertes en Territoire Loma.* Arts D'Afrique Noire, Arts Premiers 79: 19-29.

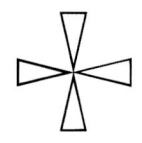

Index

Aboudoulaye, M. S., xi
Age of the Poro, 15
Age groups, 16
Aluminum, 29, 33, 34, 35, 57
Ampora, 56
Andomba, 19, 20, 54, 56
Angbai, 29, 30, 31, 44, 53
Bakorogi, 29, 34, 38
Banban, 56
Bassa, 15
Basi ti, 20
Bili, 53
Biri, 53
Birike, 20, 53
Bo Kpoa, 19
Body masks, 19, 21, 26, 27, 30, 39, 40, 42, 43, 44, 45, 46, 47, 48, 49, 52
Boys' Poro masks, 17, 22, 23, 24, 37, 45, 46, 48, 49, 52, 53, 54, 58, 59, 60, 63
Brass, 34, 35, 57
Bush Spirit, 15, 16, 17, 21, 28, 30, 32, 34, 42, 44, 57, 59, 60, 61
Buzogi, 31, 34
Circumcision, 26, 30, 53, 55, 57
Colors, meanings of, in Poro art
    Red, 20, 21, 22, 23, 24, 27, 42, 43, 48, 49
    White, 29, 35,38
Dan, 15, 16, 19, 26, 37, 52, 53, 54, 56, 57
Dazoe, 20, 55
Dubaia, 56
Elders' Poro masks, 16,19, 20, 23,24,26, 29, 31, 33, 41, 42, 50, 52, 55
Esoteric knowledge, 15, 16, 19, 54
Face masks, 15
Koranko Territory in Sierra Leone and Guinea, 17, 18
Language groups in Guinea, 25
Forehead masks, 15
Ga masks, 19
Gah' body masks, 15, 16, 19, 54 (*See* Body masks)
Gbandi, 15, 19, 22, 25, 35, 38, 53, 54, 55, 57
Gbangbe, 19, 20, 54, 55
Gbangbami, 19, 20, 54
Gbongbane, 19, 20
Gio, 37, 57
Gola, 15
Grade, 19, 24, 34, 35, 36, 38, 52, 57
Guinea Coast, 15, 26, 37
Gɛ, 19, 20, 53, 54
Gɛ Bo, 19, 20
Hats, 20, 21

Helmet masks, 15, 30
Hierarchy, 15, 19, 26, 37, 54
Horizontal masks, 15, 27, 28, 30, 31, 32, 42, 45, 52, 53
Horns,
    Number of,
        Two-horned masks, 20,21, 29, 33, 34, 36, 39, 40, 41, 42, 44, 45, 46, 47
        Three-horned masks, 20, 21, 29, 30
        Five-horned masks, 21, 22, 44, 47, 48, 49
        Six-horned mask, 38
        Seven-horned masks, 41, 42, 43
        Twelve-horned mask 23, 24, 25
    Stylistic variations of, 50
Initiation, 16, 20, 21, 22, 30
Iron, 20, 21, 23, 24, 26, 27, 34, 35, 36
Kaolin, 35, 57
Kissi, 15, 17, 18, 19, 22, 34, 35, 36, 53, 54, 55
Kissie pennies, 34, 35
Kolou Zowoi, 20, 55
Komah'h 20
Kome, 19, 20, 54, 55
Komé, 61
Komebon, 19, 20 54
Kometigi,19, 20
Kono, 15, 17, 18, 26, 52, 54, 57
Koranko, 16-27, 30, 38-52
Koranko territory in Sierra Leone and Guinea, 17, 18, 25
Kpelle, 15, 25, 35, 38, 52, 53, 54, 55, 56, 57
Kwo Wale, 35-36
Landai, 30-33, 53
Language groups in Guinea, 25
Levels of Poro, 15, 16, 19-23, 29, 30, 34, 38, 53
Limba, 19, 60, 62
Local names for Poro, 15, 19, 20
Lokko, 56
Loma, 15, 17-20, 22, 23, 25, 27, 29-31, 29-40, 42, 44, 45, 48, 50, 52-55, 57 (*See* Toma)
Loma-Mowly, 55
Mã, 20, 26, 55
Mã Da Ba, 30, 57
Mano, 15, 19, 26, 52-57
Masgui, 20, 26, 27, 34
Masks, 15-19, 20-24, 26-57
Masking traditions, 15, 16, 26, 54, 55

63

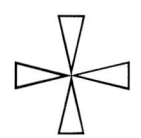

Masquerades, 15
Medicine, 15, 19, 20, 23, 26, 34-36, 41-49, 54, 57
Men's Poro, 16, 19, 21-23, 30, 35, 42-45, 47-49, 54
Mende, 54, 56
Metal, 15, 23, 28-31, 34, 37, 45, 47, 57
Metal strips, 34, 57
Metals as an indicator of grade level, 33-35, 57
Nyangbai, 44 (*See Angbai*)
Nyenne, 19, 20, 54, 55
ŋina, 20, 55
Oaths, 17, 29
Okobuzogui, 28, 56
Patterns, scarification 16, 21-22, 54
Poison, 16, 23, 26, 57
Polo, 20, 26, 55
Pölögii, 20, 26, 55
Poro,
    Basic structure of, 15-16
    Masks of, 15-19, 20-24, 26-57
    Native terminology for, 19-20
    Secrets, 16, *(See* Secrecy)
Published Examples of Koranko masks, 39-49
River God, 30, 37, 57, 58
Sacred Bush, 16, 20, 26, 27, 29, 30, 33, 37, 53, 54, 55
Sacred Grove, *See* Sacred Bush
Sacrifice, 15, 16, 20, 21, 26, 28, 29, 55, 61
Scarification, 16, 21-22, 54

Secrecy
    Penalty for revealing secrets, 16-17
    Secret codes, 16
    Secret language, 16
    Secret names, 16
    Secret signs, 56
Senufo, 15, 39, 53
Signs of West African secret societies, 56
    Sign of the *Ampora*, 56
    Sign of the *Andomba*, 56
Social-religious-political role of Poro, 15-16
Spirit of the Waters, 33, 41, 64
Stone, 15, 36-38, 57
Stone mask, 15, 36-38, 57
Style, 15-17, 28-30, 36, 38-41, 44, 47, 50, 52, 54
Stylistic Variations, 55
Temne, 17, 18, 39, 54
Terracotta, 27, 35-36
Toma, 15, 17-19, 21-23, 25-34, 38-41, 44, 47, 48, 50, 52, 54, 57
Toma territory, 18, 25
Torma, 56
Traditional religion, 15, 17
Unworn masks, 15, 23,, 24, 26, 27, 37, 52, 57
Vai, 54
Water spirits, 30, 37, 57, 58
White, color, 29, 35, 38
Zo, 16, 19, 20, 28, 33, 34, 35, 54, 55